Roger Rawlinson

Keyboard Quickly and Easily

KEYBOARD QUICKLY AND EASILY

GAYNOR ATTWOOD
Department of Education, Bristol Polytechnic
and
HAROLD JOPSON

STANLEY
THORNES

First published in 1986 by:
McGraw-Hill Book Company

Reprinted in 1995 by:
Stanley Thornes (Publishers) Ltd
Ellenborough House
Wellington Street
CHELTENHAM GL50 1YD
United Kingdom

Reprinted 1995

A catalogue record for this book is available from the British Library.

ISBN 0 7487 2198 3

Phototypeset by Gecko Limited, Bicester, Oxon.
Printed and bound in Great Britain

CONTENTS

Introduction

This book is designed as a basic learning text for all who wish to master the QWERTY keyboard for whatever reason. Whether for personal or business typewriting skill in the traditional sense, or for word processing or data/computer input, it provides material so structured and sequenced that students may proceed through it by a 'fast route' or a slow one, and add on the essentials of data/computer input if they wish to do so.

The guidance of a good teacher is never to be despised, but students who are sufficiently motivated and determined, can use the book as a self-teaching manual with every prospect of success.

Notes to teachers

The book makes individual and group work relatively easy to plan. For keen and intelligent students the fast route may be all that is needed to gain rapid mastery of the keyboard. Exercises 1 to 26 offer the minimum keyboard training, while the extension units may be used as required. For students with more time, or who find the keyboarding skill less easy to acquire, the extra practice passages should also be attempted. Complete accuracy should be encouraged from the start, especially for those students requiring data/computer input skills.

Notes to students

Careful, regular and determined practice is the secret of keyboard mastery. But it is necessary to practise the right skills, and these demand good posture, correct and effortless movement, and the coordination of hand and brain. Study the section below on 'Keys to Keyboarding' and refer back to it constantly as your learning proceeds. Read all instructions (there are not many) and obey them. You should learn the keyboard in quite a short space of time.

Commonly Misspelt words

(Set tab stops 15, 35 and 55 from the left-hand margin.

abbreviate	accommodation	acknowledge	advertisement
address	bankrupt	beneficial	budget
bureau	business	calendar	circular
committee	conference	criticism	deficit
definitely	development	disagree	disapprove
eligible	emergency	enormous	exercise
expenditure	financial	forfeit	frequency
guarantee	honorary	illegal	immediate
independent	leisure	literature	maintenance
memorandum	necessary	occasion	opposite
peculiar	possession	procedure	questionnaire
quiet	relief	restaurant	separate
signature	surprise	temperature	temporary
typical	usually	unusually	vehicle

Common Short Words

it he if do so at an of to me
is on by or in no up we us be

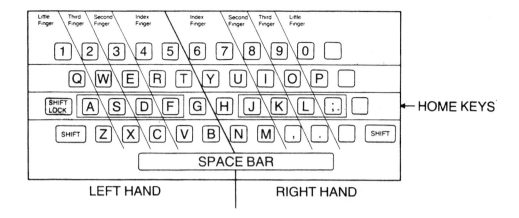

LEFT HAND | RIGHT HAND

Keys to Keyboarding

All skills depend on highly developed coordination between body and brain. This is especially true of keyboarding. Accuracy and speed can only be maximized through typing by touch, ie, keeping the eyes on the copy (*what* is being typed) in order to maintain complete concentration, and making all the right movements (*how* it is being typed) automatically.

The keys to good keyboarding are *position, movement and concentration.*

Position

The movements of the fingers from the home keys (see diagram on page 3) are directional, and to get the directions right it is necessary to start always from the right place.

1 Keep the fingers hovering above the home keys. Movements are always away from those keys and back.
2 Bend the fingers at the knuckles so that the ball of the finger strikes the key.
3 Have the forearms roughly level with the keyboard; the chair must be at the correct height for this.
4 Keep the back straight and both feet firmly on the floor.

Drills

Double Letter Drills

letter setter mitten kitten hotter jotter
fellow yellow bellow mellow zipper kipper
supper rubble wobble tariff tunnel called
sudden summer hammer barred potted cotton

Common Prefixes

pre -   present predict prepare preside preview prefect

pro -   protein provide propose product procure protest

ex   -   extreme extinct extract expense excuses exploit

Common Suffixes

tion -   station fiction section caution suction caption

ment -   segment augment element ferment torment fitment

ing -   storing fitting setting staying leaving getting

Movement

The most skilful keyboard operators are those whose movements are minimal.

1 Depress each key with the correct finger.
2 Move finger and hand no further than is necessary to reach the key.
3 Keep the rest of the body (including arms and head) still.

Concentration

Eyes on the copy all the time. Keep reading the material that is being typed. Do not move head or eyes to look anywhere else.

Signs and symbols on the top line of the keyboard vary from machine to machine, therefore they have been omitted from the keyboard diagrams.

Consolidation Exercises

To instal a 28-pin ROM chip: remove the ROM from its antistatic packaging. The 'notch' on the chip must face away from the keyboard, the chip should be inserted in any of the sockets IC88, IC100 or IC101.

In 1833 Charles Babbage (Professor of Mathematics at Cambridge University, England) dreamed of building a computer. Alas, he never completed the computer he called the "Analytical Engine".

The size of A4 paper is 210 x 297 mm. A5 landscape paper is 210 x 148 mm and A5 portrait is 148 x 210 mm. There are 10 pica characters and 12 elite characters to the inch.

Since the on/off principle only allows for two positions, these are shown in computer work as 1 and 0.

A dot matrix printer is more expensive than a thermal printer but it prints more legibly. Daisy-wheel printers are expensive but print very clearly.

Serial interfaces send or receive 'bytes' of information one bit at a time. Parallel interfaces allow all 'eight bits in a byte' to travel in or out of a computer at the same time, along eight separate wires.

In 1620 the Pilgrim Fathers sailed from Plymouth on board the "Mayflower" and eventually landed in Cape Cod.

In 1750 the journey from London to Edinburgh took 10 to 12 days. By 1830 it took 50 hours; by 1850 18 hours and by 1855 13 hours. Do you know how long it takes today?

It was the committee's immediate intention to seek accommodation beneficial to the patients. The questionnaire drawn up at the recent conference had definitely assisted in establishing the patients' perception of their needs. These would be met in the new development, and the necessary maintenance staff could be recruited.

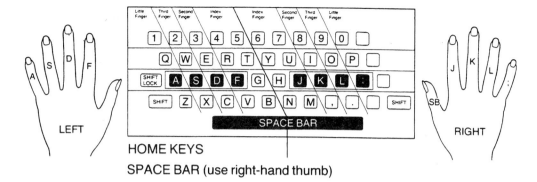

LEFT

RIGHT

HOME KEYS

SPACE BAR (use right-hand thumb)

General Instructions

Unless otherwise instructed use A4 paper, set margins of 15 and 85 elite, or 10 and 72 pica, and use double line-spacing.

Type each line until you get it completely accurate.

Before starting, read 'Keys to Keyboarding'.

Exercise 1   New Keys asdf;lkj

```
asdf;lkjasdf;lkjasdf;lkjasdf;lkj
asdf;lkjasdf;lkjasdf;lkjasdf;lkj

asdf ;lkj asdf ;lkj asdf ;lkj asdf ;lkj
asdf ;lkj asdf ;lkj asdf ;lkj asdf ;lkj

as ad af as ad af as ad af
al ak aj al ak aj al ak aj

sad fad lad sad fad lad sad fad lad
dad jak alf dad jak alf dad jak alf
add all ask add all ask add all ask

fall lass fads lads alas adds
as sad as dad; as sad as dad;
```

```
5  CLS
10 PRINT "MORTGAGE PROGRAM"
15 INPUT "What is the size of your mortgage in £'s",M
20 INPUT "What is the amount of your monthly repayment",R
25 INPUT "WHAT is the interest rate as a %",I
30 LET T=0
35 REPEAT
40 M=M+(M*I)/100-12*R
45 LET T=T+1
50 UNTIL M<(12*R)
55 N%=M/R
60 PRINT "Your mortgage will be repaid after"
65 PRINT T," years",N%," months"
70 END
```

Exercise 2

Remember: Eyes on copy

```
as; ad; af; as; ad; af;
al; ak; aj; al; ak; aj;

kaj sal daj lak kas jad
kaj sal daj lak kas jad

jads kads fads jads kads fads
jads kads fads jads kads fads

flask salad flask salad flask salad

salad asks alf; salad asks alf;
alas a sad lad; alas a sad lad;
```

The following exercises are computer programs. This type of work requires complete accuracy.

Remember: Spaces should be as the copy and where you see a zero you should type a numeric '0' and never the capital letter 'O'.

```
10 REM COIN TOSSING PROGRAM
20 CLS
30 LET H=0
40 LET T=0
50 PRINT:PRINT "How many throws?"
60 INPUT N
70 FOR C=1 TO N
80 LET X=RND(1)
90 IF X<=0.5 THEN LET H=H+1
100 IF X>0.5 THEN LET T=T+1
110 NEXT C
120 PRINT "Number of heads = ";H
130 PRINT "Number of tails = ";T
```

```
10 CLS
15 @%=&20209
20 PRINT "FAHRENHEIT TO CELSIUS CONVERSION"
30 INPUT "Enter start and finish temperatures",S,F
40 LET I=1
50 IF S>F THEN I=-1
60 FOR TEMP=S TO F STEP I
70 LET C=(TEMP-32)*5/9
80 PRINT;TEMP;"  DEG F=";C;"  DEG C"
90 NEXT TEMP
100 END
```

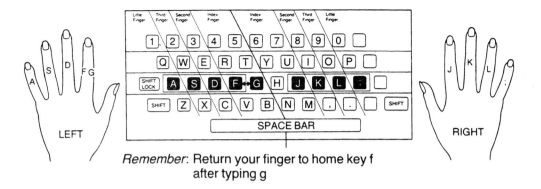

Remember: Return your finger to home key f
after typing g

Exercise 3   New Key g

```
fgf fgf fgf fgf fgf fgf fgf fgf

gas lag gad kag sag
jag gal gak fag dag

gala glad gall saga
gala glad gall saga

lags jags gaff flag glass
lags jags gaff flag glass

lag a glass; lag a glass;
a gas saga; a gas saga; a gas saga;
```

Exercises

Task 1 Type the heading OPEN PUNCTUATION and then type the following sentences in that style.

Task 2 Type the heading FULL PUNCTUATION and then type the sentences in that style.

1   The abbreviation km/h stands for kilometres per hour.

2   For further information on the EEC write to EEC Information Unit, 11th Floor, 13 Millbank St, London SW1P 4QU or telephone 01 211 7060.

3   The area of a rectangle is calculated by length multiplied by width (l x w): for the school's toy box that was, 2 m x 1.5 m, giving an area of 3 sq m.

4   Every performance or publication of J M Barrie's "Peter Pan" secures a royalty for the work of Great Ormond Street Hospital for Sick Children, London.

5   "Oh no! They would make me grow up. I want to stay a little boy always, and have fun!" cried Peter Pan.

6   Notice is hereby given that the AGM of J Bee & Sons plc will be held at the Head Office, 51 King Square, Birmingham on 21 June 1987 at 1200 hours.

7   One A4 page of typing can contain approximately 2 000 characters. If one cassette tape can store 250 000 characters, how many A4 pages would this cassette tape hold?

8   The new luxury estate "Green Lawns" contained a range of 3 and 4 bedroom split-level houses and bungalows. Prices range from £42,000 to £65,000.

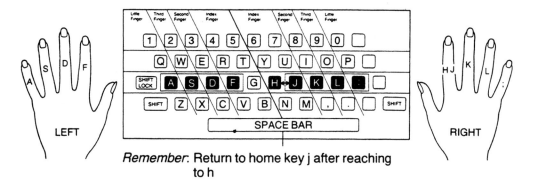

Remember: Return to home key j after reaching to h

Exercise 4 New Key h

jhj jhj jhj jhj jhj jhj jhj jhj

had has ash hak aha
aha jah dah lah hal

gash dash hall half lash
gash dash hall half lash

slash flash shall slash flash shall
halls shall halls shall halls shall

add a dash; add a dash; add a dash;
a glad lad adds a dash; a glad lass;

Extra Practice

asdf ;lkj asdf ;lkj asdf ;lkj asdf ;lkj

fgf jhj fgf jhj fgf jhj fgf jhj

asdfg ;lkjh asdfg ;lkjh asdfg ;lkjh

half a glass flask half a glass flask

shall ash fall shall ash fall shall ash fall

Key h 6

Note the Following Display Rules

1 Postcodes are always typed without punctuation.

2 When using a twelve-hour clock, times always have a full stop separating hours from minutes.

3 When using a twenty-four hour clock, times are always represented by four figures without space or stop.

4 No full stops are required on the following occasions:
   (a) after abbreviations in the metric system
   (b) after the 'p' when used as an abbreviation for pence
   (c) after roman numerals.
   The only exception to this rule is when these abbreviations are found at the end of a sentence.

5 Numbers of five digits or more.
   In open punctuation the comma, normally used to separate groups of three figures, is replaced by a space. Four digit numbers may be typed with or without a space. When typing money, comma(s) must be inserted whether open or full punctuation is used.

Examples

	FULL PUNCTUATION	OPEN PUNCTUATION
1	SN3 4PX	SN3 4PX
2	9.30 p.m.	9.30 pm
3	2130 hrs.	2130 hrs
4	10 cm 60p Henry VIII	10 cm 60p Henry VIII
5	10,327 1,286 or 1286 £82,432.97	10 327 1 286 or 1286 £82,432.97

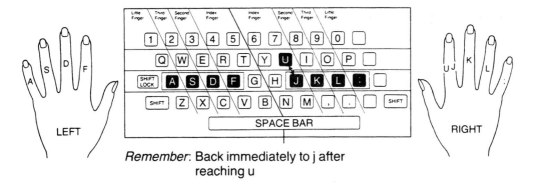

Remember: Back immediately to j after reaching u

Exercise 5   New Letter u

Reaching to the top row

juj juj juj juj juj juj juj juj

jud jug jud jug jud jug
dud sud lug dug hug sud
usk ugh usk ugh usk ugh

full dull gush hush full dull gush hush
lush husk gull hull lush husk gull hull

sulk fuss haul hulk sulk fuss haul hulk
huff jugs suss glug huff jugs suss glug

fluff sulks laugh fluff sulks laugh
fluff sulks laugh fluff sulks laugh

Extension Unit 4

Punctuation

There are two main methods of punctuating work:

OPEN PUNCTUATION   This method uses the minimum of punctuation. It includes only the punctuation necessary to make the meaning clear.

FULL PUNCTUATION   This is the method where all punctuation marks are included.

These methods of punctuation can be best compared by looking at the following examples.

	FULL PUNCTUATION	OPEN PUNCTUATION
1	1st January, 1987	1st January 1987
2	Mr. S. Holliday	Mr S Holliday
3	Mrs. J. Bressington, 123, Brislington Rd., BRISTOL, Avon. BS4 4RT	Mrs J Bressington 123 Brislington Rd BRISTOL Avon BS4 4RT
4	The meeting was held at the B.B.C. headquarters at 12.30 p.m. on Wednesday, 2nd March, 1986.	The meeting was held at the BBC headquarters at 12.30 pm on Wednesday, 2nd March 1986.

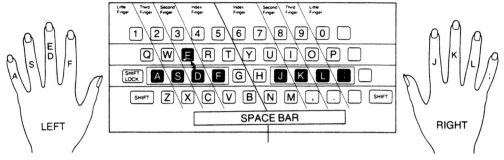

Remember: Eyes on copy

Exercise 6   New Letter e

ded ded ded ded ded ded ded ded

fed jed led fed jed led
lea sea eel lea sea eel
leg due hue leg due hue

eggs desk safe duel fuel shed
deal deaf fell gale dale fake
feed seed heed keel feel seek

flake heads sleek fudge glade
sheds adage eased deals fluke

ladle fused shade guess judge
lease glued shake geese fudge

sausage juggled luggage
sausage juggled luggage

Using equal margins, type the following paragraphs including the headings.

BLOCKED PARAGRAPH

Many people learn the keyboard and become very proficient. Their work is accurate and attractively displayed, but unfortunately their spelling, punctuation and ability to construct good sentences are often poor.

INDENTED PARAGRAPH

Work typed or processed accurately from the point of view of the keyboard skill, is unsatisfactory if spelling or language use is poor. At best it looks amateurish; at worst the meaning is not what was intended. "The girl had difficulty in getting the male through the letter box", has its amusing aspect, but reflects rather poorly on the typist!

HANGING PARAGRAPH

If you are to maintain a high level of accuracy in your finished work, it will be necessary for you to develop your proofreading skills. Proofreading is the means of identifying all errors in your work. If you are using a word processor or a computer, you can proofread on the VDU (visual display unit).

Extra Practice

```
use age leg keg use age leg keg
eke see uke fee eke see uke fee

dell fell hell sell kale lead deaf fuse
less ease held duke jude duel leek fuel

sad gulls shall sulk   sad gulls shall sulk

she used less eggs   she used less eggs

dad has a full glass   dad has a full glass

he used less luggage   he used less luggage

he shall seal all deeds   he shall seal all deeds

he had sausages she had eggs   he had sausages she had eggs
```

Extension Unit 3

Paragraphs

Types of Paragraphs

Paragraphs may be displayed in three forms:

BLOCKED   All lines begin at the left-hand margin.

INDENTED   The first line of each paragraph begins five spaces in from the left-hand margin.

HANGING   The first line of each paragraph begins at the left-hand margin, all other lines being three spaces in from the left-hand margin.

Spacing between paragraphs

When typing in single line-spacing, *always* turn up two lines between paragraphs.

When typing in other than single line-spacing, turn up an extra line only when typing blocked paragraphs.

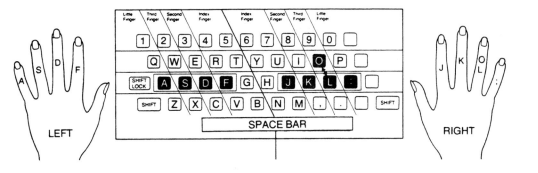

LEFT   RIGHT

Exercise 7   New Letter o

lol lol lol lol lol lol lol lol

log jog dog hog log jog dog hog
sod hod oak fog sod hod oak fog
old ago off ado old ago off ado

load loss foal dole goal also
hole gold hold joke soak hook

golf fold oaks sold loaf sago
doll good food hoof look fool

hello lodge floss gloss house louse
flood holes goals folds shoal lasso
shoes foals dolls goods doles loads

Using the spacing and layout as required for general keyboarding purposes, type the following exercise at least twice.

1   Do not break the glass <u>except in an emergency</u>.

2   You must post this letter today! It is mid-day - time for lunch.

3   I'll give you all £5.00 to spend.

4   "Who's been sitting in my chair?" said baby bear.

5   Follow the M5 to the M5/M4 junction at <u>Almondsbury</u>, north of Bristol.

6   The best-known cloud form is cumulus: great towering masses of white "cotton-wool".

7   Please supply 6 dozen items, catalogue number 67/89/A @ £2.20 per dozen (less 5% trade discount).

8   The book costs £9.50 (including postage and packing) from Crosby, Hannay & Baines plc.

9   50 + 50 - 25 = 75
    82 + 28 - 35 = 75
    12 x 10 - 45 = 75

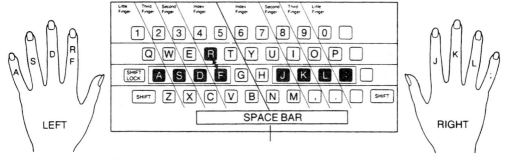

Re-read: 'Keys to Keyboarding'

Exercise 8   New Letter r

frf frf frf frf frf frf frf frf

far for fur far for fur
her are jar her are jar

our ore oar our ore oar
red ear her red ear her

fear fare free fore fear fare free fore
role hard lard jeer role hard lard jeer

hear door rude gear hear door rude gear
jerk roll raja road jerk roll raja road

grade sugar dread sheer floor juror large
fresh greed dress rakes freed heard fakes

Key r   11

$	dollar or computer string	The prize was $500.
#	can stand for number or computer hash	Actor #1
%	percentage	The service charge was 20%.
?	question mark	Why? When? Where?

For a decimal point use a full stop.

There may also be square brackets available, greater than or less than signs, and a variety of fractions.

If your keyboard does not have an exclamation mark or a conventional division sign, these are created by using a combination of characters eg
  ! (apostrophe, then backspace, then full stop)
  ÷ (colon, then backspace, then hyphen)

Extra Practice

sore dark fork lark sore dark fork lark

frugal shakes dealer darker roller feared

he sold good shoes he sold good shoes

she graded her goods for sale she graded her goods for sale

he had four dark doors for sale he had four dark doors for sale

she used her large red dresses for rags

he heard her ask for a large jar of sugar

"	quotation marks or inverted commas	"Hello" he said.
/	solidus	The reference on the letter was 123/GA/86.
@	at	6 computers @ £300
£	pound	The jacket cost £49.
_	underscore or underline	<u>Underscore correctly</u>.
&	ampersand	James & Son plc
'	apostrophe or single quotation mark	The teacher's car was a Fiat. Michelle enjoyed reading 'Watership Down'.
(	opening bracket	
)	closing bracket	The price (quoted to the customer) was inclusive of VAT and service charge.
-	hyphen or dash	hyphen off-peak, part-time dash Prince Charles dedicated it to all employees - past and present.
-	minus (if not available use hyphen)	
+	plus	3 + 2 - 1 = 4
=	equal	
*	asterisk or computer multiplication	One of the most famous comets is named Halley's* comet: *Edmund Halley (1656-1742).
:	a colon	

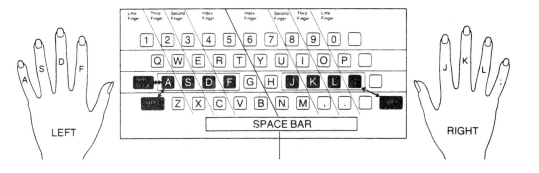

The Shift Key and Shift Lock

So far only lower case letters have been used, but the next exercise requires capital letters. This necessitates operating the shift keys or shift lock.

Directions for Shift Lock

1 Find the SHIFT LOCK on your keyboard and depress it.
2 Type the following:

JOE FRED FREDA ADA DORA LAURA SARA

Note: When the shift lock is down, all the letters are capitals.

3 Release the shift lock.

If only one capital letter is required in a word, then the shift keys are used.

Directions for capital letters

1 Find the shift keys (one on the left and one on the right).
2 Use the left-hand shift key when typing a right-hand letter and vice versa.
3 Depress the appropriate shift key and keep it down while typing the letter. Release the shift key immediately. *Make sure your fingers return to the home keys.*
4 Type the following. The first line requires the operation of the *right-hand* shift key; the second line requires the *left-hand* and the third requires both.

Ada Freda Sarah Dale Dora Russell

Joe Les Laura Harold Kraford Holford Jaffa

Douglas Laura Sarah Holford Freda Joe Dale Harold

Extension Unit 2

Special Characters and Signs

The signs and special characters that are largely upper case symbols on the number keybank – though a few appear elsewhere – need to be mastered and typed competently by touch. If this is not done, then whenever one of them is required, the continuity of the typing and the concentration of the operator will be marred by a visual search! Moreover, several of the signs – notably quotation marks, apostrophe and hyphen – are used frequently.

Unfortunately, the location of the signs and special characters varies on different QWERTY keyboards, and students must familiarize themselves with the positions on their own machines – bearing in mind that a change to another machine will necessitate some re-learning. It is necessary to practise finger reaches suitable for the particular keyboard. For example, if the quotation mark is the upper case sign on figure 2, then practise

    s (press shift key) " (release shift key) s
    on the page will appear
    s"s

The rule for developing correct finger reaches is 'confidence, ease, and economy of movement'. The reach that feels most comfortable, and involves the least movement of hand and finger, is correct.

Remember it is *essential* to return the hand to its position over the home keys *without looking*.

Important

Correct layout of typescript gives the clearest and easiest communication. Alongside the following list are given examples of the correct display.

It is imperative that material for data/computer entry be keyed in *exactly* as given. Even a space in the wrong place will result in the incorrect meaning.

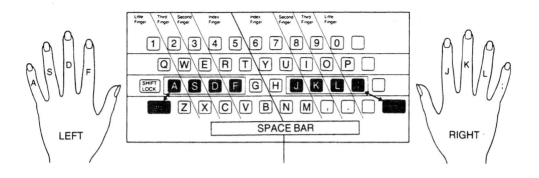

Exercise 9   Introducing the Shift Key

aAa sSs dDd fFf gGg aAa sSs dDd fFf

lLl kKk jJj hHh lLl kKk jJj hHh gGg

eEe rRr uUu eEe rRr uUu eEe rRr uUu

Asa Ada Sal Sue Des Fea Gae Ele
Lou Leo Hal Haj Kea Kes Jed Ure

Fred Dora Safa Rose Jake Dale Olga

Freda Laura Rhoda Hedda Flora Ollie
Les; Freda; Dora; all had good food

Extra Practice

The Dragon Hotel accommodates 66 guests whereas the Hotel Commodore can cater for 616 guests.

There was a woman who had 7 husbands; each husband had 7 cats and each cat had 7 kittens.

The 800 metres race was won in a time of 1 minute and 58 seconds.

The printer made 99 posters and 999 tickets for the dance on the 9th April.

The library was well stocked with over 500 books and 100 journals even though there were only 100 pupils in the school.

12 plus 34 plus 56 plus 78 equals 180.

61 plus 20 plus 31 plus 97 equals 209.

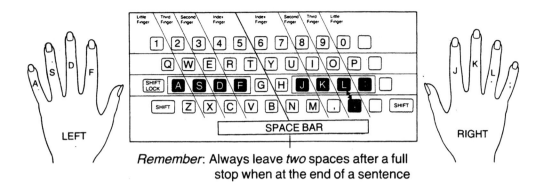

Remember: Always leave *two* spaces after a full
stop when at the end of a sentence

Exercise 10   New Key .

1.1 1.1 1.1 1.1 1.1 1.1 1.1 1.1

All lads had salad. All lads had salad.
Kes laughed as he juggled. Kes laughed as he juggled.

Safa shall seal all deeds for Laura.
Dad had sausages; Joe had eggs.

Freda graded her goods for sale.
Hal heard Dora ask for a large jar of sugar.

Joe had half a glass of ale. Joe had half a glass of ale.

Key .   15

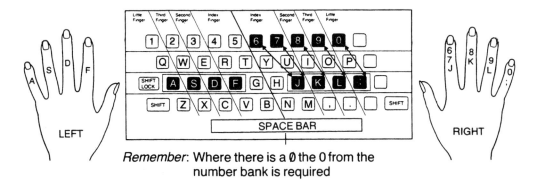

Remember: Where there is a Ø the 0 from the number bank is required

Exercise 28   New Keys 6 7 8 9 0

```
jyj jy6yj j6j jyj jy6yj j6j
j6j j6j j6j j6j j6j j6j j6j
6 yoghurts, 66 yams, 616 yeast cakes

juj ju7uj j7j juj ju7uj j7j
j7j j7j j7j j7j j7j j7j j7j
7 umbrellas, 77 unicorns, 717 unicycles

kik ki8ik k8k kik ki8ik k8k
k8k k8k k8k k8k k8k k8k k8k
8 kings, 88 knights, 818 knaves

lol lo9ol 191 lol lo9ol 191
191 191 191 191 191 191 191
9 linesmen, 99 lumbermen, 919 librarians

;p; ;pØp; ;Ø; ;p; ;pØp; ;Ø;
;Ø; ;Ø; ;Ø; ;Ø; ;Ø; ;Ø; ;Ø;
10 petunias, 100 pinks, 101 palm trees
```

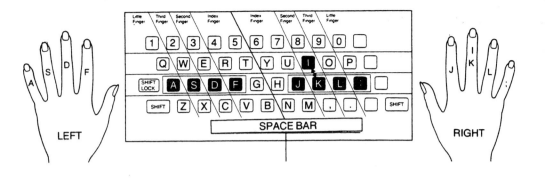

Exercise 11 New Letter i

kik kik kik kik kik kik kik kik

kid jig fig rig kid jig fig rig
his hid did rio his hid did rio
ail ire sir lie ail ire sir lie

kill kiss hill like jail said
dial girl fire dias file hide

drill grail field hike siege rifle

Ira Del Uri Eli Kia Aja

He shared her ideas. He shared her ideas.
Dad did like his free ride. Dad did like his free ride.

Extra Practice

Ravi has seat 1 in car 1 of train 1 which is standing at platform 11.

Send 22 to Lucy, 21 to John, 22 to Jeremy and 221 to Yasmin.

The motel lost 133 sheets and towels in 3 months and 13 days.

The law was passed on 14 August 1141 and not 14 November 1441 as stated in the newspaper article.

He sold 115 ice creams, 55 lollipops and 155 wafers to the crowd of 555 at the summer pop concert.

Extra Practice

fir ill oil gig fir ill oil gig

soil rail idea hire hike foil
raid hail rile jail sire aids

Jill Giles Ali; Lars Julie Lee

glides failed soiled afraid foiled shrill

He should hire a radio for his hike.
Laura said if Uri is free he should hide.

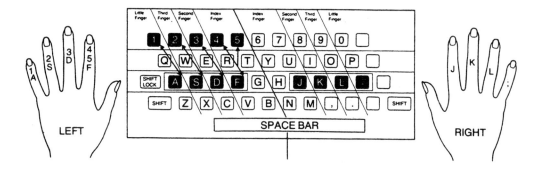

Exercise 27   New Keys 1 2 3 4 5

```
aqa aqlqa ala aqa aqlqa ala
ala ala ala ala ala ala ala
1 apple, 11 apricots, 111 aubergines


sws sw2ws s2s sws sw2ws s2s
s2s s2s s2s s2s s2s s2s s2s
2 swans, 22 seagulls, 212 swallows

ded de3ed d3d ded de3ed d3d
d3d d3d d3d d3d d3d d3d d3d
3 dogfish, 33 dolphins, 313 deep sea divers

frf fr4rf f4f frf fr4rf f4f
f4f f4f f4f f4f f4f f4f f4f
4 roads, 44 railways, 414 rally tracks

ftf ft5tf f5f ftf ft5tf f5f
f5f f5f f5f f5f f5f f5f f5f
5 tigers, 55 toads, 515 tadpoles
```

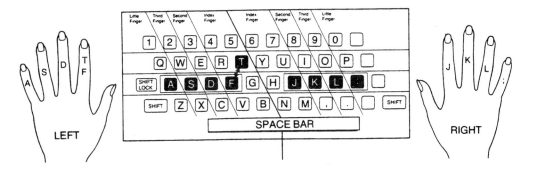

Exercise 12 New Letter t

```
frf ftf frf ftf frf ftf frf ftf
ftf ftf ftf ftf ftf ftf ftf ftf

fat fit sat sit fat fit sat sit
aft lit kit ate aft lit kit ate

flat slit tree talk kite star
tour host riot east heat tilt

the that this there their these three
the that this there their these three

She tried to tilt the seat just a little.
The lad took the letters to their addresses.
All through tea Kate talked to her little sister.
Lee thought Harold had the tools; Ruth had to use the drill.
```

Extension Unit 1

Numbers

Many students tend to neglect the number keybank, either because it is difficult and time-consuming to master, or because it is felt that the numbers may not be used very much. The first reason is unworthy of a serious student, and the second is probably untrue.

Certainly for data/computer entry an excellent skill with numbers is essential. It is necessary to achieve 100 per cent accuracy, and this must take precedence over speed.

The exercises that follow should be practised until a high degree of accuracy is attained, and it may be necessary to return to them later for final consolidation.

Extra Practice

```
hot jut let toe get hit
eat too got jot tot rat

tell date last trot kilt
fret tall drat feet tool

feast other light talks toast treat
flight throat sitter thrill little flight

though thought through throughout

Tara Kate Seta Otto Tara Kate Seta Otto

Rita ate all the toast for tea.
Arthur thought that all girls had kilts.
Teresa dislikes Ruth; she is jealous of her.
```

Extra Practice

Type the following sentences in single line-spacing, leaving one clear line space between each sentence.

There are twelve signs of the Zodiac; Aries, Taurus, Gemini, Cancer, Leo, Virgo, Libra, Scorpio, Sagittarius, Capricorn, Aquarius and Pisces.

The seven days of the week are Monday, Tuesday, Wednesday, Thursday, Friday, Saturday and Sunday.

The twelve months of the year are January, February, March, April, May, June, July, August, September, October, November and December.

Set the tabulator stops at 15, 30 and 45 characters from the left-hand margin.

Bristol	Bournemouth	Belfast
Bradford	Barnstaple	Billingham
Birmingham	Brecon	Barrow
Bolton	Brechin	Ballycastle

Returning the Carriage

From now on some sentences will be included which are more than 70 spaces long. It will, therefore, be necessary to return the carriage to the left-hand margin (unless using a word processor) in order to complete the typing.

To return the carriage

1 On a manual machine – push the carriage return lever smartly but smoothly with the left hand. Return the fingers to the home keys.

2 On electric and electronic machines – use the little finger of the right hand to depress the 'return' key. Return fingers to the home keys.

3 On a word processor – the carriage return is automatic, but when a 'hard return' is required, it is necessary to press the 'return' key.

Type the following:

```
At Telford Laura talked all through tea although Stuart
tried to shelter to eat the sausages.
```

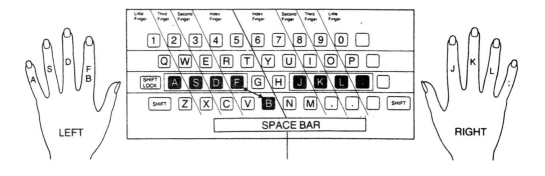

LEFT

RIGHT

Exercise 26   New Letter b

```
fvf fbf fvf fbf fvf fbf fvf fbf
fbf fbf fbf fbf fbf fbf fbf fbf
```

```
fab fob big bat web orb
but boy beg bye ban bib
```

```
bank bury back club able busy
ibex book bomb bell robe jibe
```

```
public bother member rabbit bright
buying bather treble begins baboon
sobbed wobble gobble rubber pebble
```

```
librarian neighbour obsession bungalows
```

Both boys remembered to buy a birthday present for Rebecca.

Brighton and Bournemouth are both seaside resorts on the south coast of England, but while Brighton is bracing and has many day trippers, Bournemouth is relaxing and boasts a larger number of retired residents.

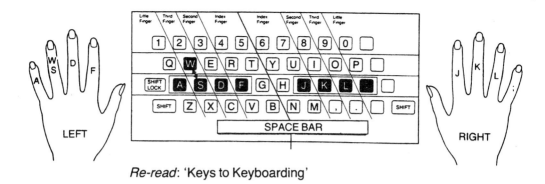

Re-read: 'Keys to Keyboarding'

Exercise 13   New Letter w

sws sws sws sws sws sws sws sws

was law jaw was law jaw
wit wet two wit wet two

wife tows owls were with weed
whet what wish wood wake week

sweet water shows draws straw swell
throw waste water allow await world

The waiter asked Walter whether he had water.
Sarah Wills wore a wool dress with her straw hat.

Wilfred wrote a letter; he asked Rhoda whether she would go.
The weather was good so the two girls with their dog Otto set
out to walk through the hills.

Extra Practice

The prizes for the waltz championship, held at the Plaza, were itemized in the programme.

A dozen dazzling prizes were offered for the pizza contest held at the Zoological Gardens in Zurich.

Set the tab stops at 20, 40 and 60 characters from your left-hand margin.

COUNTRIES

United Kingdom	Afghanistan	Finland
Kenya	China	Mexico
Nigeria	Denmark	Canada
Switzerland	Portugal	Yugoslavia
Italy	United States	India
Greece	Tanzania	New Zealand

Extra Practice

how who war how who war
low raw few low raw few

wall will well walk wait wise
slow flow glow flaw grow flew

where threw swells awaits waits

sweater whether wallows weather hallows shallow

Wells Wales Towie Lewes Wells Wales Towie Lewes

Giles showed his wife where the owls were.
Luke Watts will walk to the well for water.
Faith wished to read well so she tried hard.
The weather was wet so we sheltered for a while.

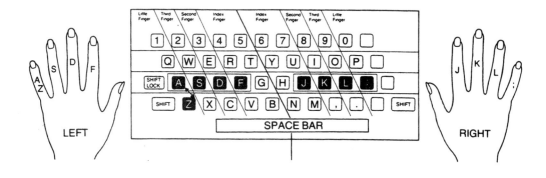

Exercise 25   New Letter z

aza aza aza aza aza aza aza aza

azd fez zip zoo zax zee zap zim
azd fez zip zoo zax zee zap zim

maze zinc size lazy zone zero
czar quiz whiz zoom laze oozy

fizzy fuzzy jazzy dizzy fizzy
crazy dozen azure prize sized

fizzle dazzle nozzle piazza puzzle muzzle
frozen zephyr wizard zipper zodiac nuzzle

grizzle horizon zealous outsize squeeze zoology

The maze quiz suited the lazy girl; she enjoyed doing the
difficult puzzle.

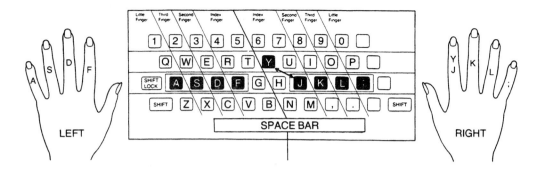

Exercise 14   New Letter y

juj jyj juj jyj juj jyj juj jyj
jyj jyj jyj jyj jyj jyj jyj jyj

jay joy lay ray way shy
thy yes why guy you try

they whey year yell lady your
easy yard dyes eyes yoke holy

jelly dairy witty yeast daily fairy

Gary liked the girl who wore the yellow dress.
Harry asked the shy lady why the girl yelled all day.

The dealer at York yesterday sold hats with large yellow
feathers to the fellows.

Extra Practice

```
live vote view move wavy jive
oval gave cave navy volt veer

crave gravy avoid heavy cover verse
evoke liver pivot never woven seven

vertex cravat convey silver favour heaven
motive octavo thieve tavern sliver values
```

Set the tab stops at 15, 30 and 45 from the left-hand margin.

```
overdose    overdraw    overgrow
overhear    overlook    overrate
overseas    overstay    overcome
```

Extra Practice

yew eye key fry dye say
aye hay dye toy lay yet

sway yeti yolk fray yoke guys

fully folly holly ditty kitty witty
youth yield loyal style study jolly

yellow styled easily friary faulty

holiday lottery loyalty greatly Tuesday

Kay had dry eyes yet she still looked sad.
The yellow dye was far too dark for the fairy dress.
Terry said that his holiday at York started yesterday.

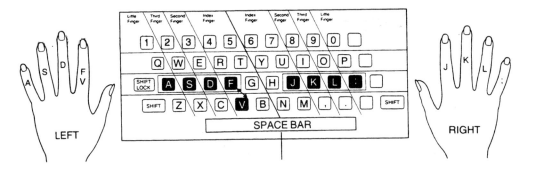

Exercise 24   New Letter v

fvf fvf fvf fvf fvf fvf fvf fvf

vat vet rev vex van vim
via eve vie ave vow via

five love save rove pave very
wave ever hive cove have over

divide convex eleven volume native
valley savage review pelvis sleeve

flavour, revolve, removes, violent, vehicle,

Every villa in Le Verdon has a lovely view over the cove.
Vivien said her favourite flavour had a very savoury tang.

David said that he did not remove the valve from the van, so
it must have been Clive.

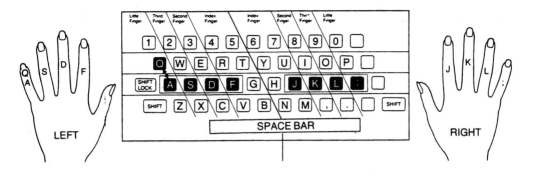

Exercise 15   New Letter q

aqa aqa aqa aqa aqa aqa aqa aqa
aqu aqu aqu aqu aqu aqu aqu aqu

aqua quid quay quit quad aqua

quote quilt quiet queue quest quite

quarter quarrel qualify equator quadrat

The queue waited quietly for the last quarter to start.
The quiet lady followed her quest to the equator to look
for quail.

Yesterday the girls took their guests for a quiet day at
the forest. It was eerie as the trees swayed slightly
while the foliage hid the daylight.

Extra Practice

Using the tab, set points 20 and 40 along from the left-hand margin.

fast,	faster,	fastest,
long,	longer,	longest,
many,	more,	most,
old,	older,	oldest,
little,	less,	least,

Using the tab, set points 25 and 50 along from the left-hand margin.

again and again,	neck and neck,	such and such,
spick and span,	odds and ends,	this and that,
hue and cry,	up and away,	fair and square,
wear and tear,	touch and go,	free and easy,

Extra Practice

```
equal quake quart queer quell quill
quota quirk squat squid squad quoit

quarry squire squall queasy equity squeal

require requite request squashy liquefy
qualify quality quester quilter .quitter
```

The squire required a qualified quilter.
The quality of the dress was good so we took two.
It was queer to feel the earthquake at the Equator.
In Quito he requested a squeaky squirrel for the quiet squaw.

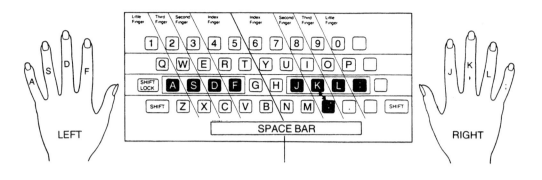

Exercise 23　　New Key ,

k,k k,k k,k k,k k,k k,k k,k k,k k,k

Count one, two, three, four, and six.

The colours were green, red, orange, yellow and purple.

The shop sold wellingtons, shoes, slippers, sandals and mules.

On the shopping list were carrots, celery, leeks, marrow,
onions and potatoes.

We went on a train, ship, lorry, aeroplane, car and truck to
reach our destination.

There were dentists, chemists, artists, farmers, joiners,
teachers, postmen and shop workers at the meeting.

The hockey team was selected with care, for the school needed
a win. Penelope, Tina, Xena and Rosemary were in defence,
keeping the opposition out.

Key ,

Using the Tabulator

The tabulator is used to stop the carriage at a pre-set point, eg, when typing columns or indenting the first line of a paragraph.

It will be helpful to use the machine handbook to assist in locating the tabulator keys. There are three – the TAB KEY, the TAB SET, and the TAB CLEAR.

Directions

1 Locate and press the TAB KEY or bar. The carriage should move right along from margin to margin. If it stops short of the margin, it will be because there are already tabs set. Press the TAB CLEAR each time the carriage stops. This clears the tabulator.

2 Set the left-hand margin at 10. Move the carriage along to 20, 30, 40, 50, and 60, pressing the TAB SET at each point.

3 Return the carriage to the left-hand margin. Move to the pre-set points by pressing the TAB KEY five times.

4 Now type the following, starting at the left-hand margin and moving to the start of each column by using the TAB KEY:

```
Faith     Sarah     Kate      Louise    Hilary    Althea
Gary      Stuart    Walter    Harry     Giles     Gerald
```

The tabulator can be used on many occasions, some of which are introduced in the pages that follow.

Extra Practice

```
apex crux hoax axle jinx onyx
taxi flex minx ilex axes waxy

helix index latex maxim waxen xenia
toxic unfix relax proxy oxide mixer

climax elixir exempt expand expose galaxy
prefix excite exodus expect luxury sphinx

context maximum example perplex extreme
sextant express textile sixteen fixture
```

The maximum allowed in the orchestra was extended to include six extra saxophones and six extra trumpets.

The exiled lady relaxed in the luxurious expanse of the mansion in the town of Xanadu.

Exercise 16

Type the following sentences after setting the tab stop five characters along from the left-hand margin stop. Before starting each sentence remember to press the tab key.

Jerry Ellis said that the weather was so foul that the girls would stay for a little while.

At a quarter to eight daily the lorry left the yard so that it would get to Fallowfield at three.

The girl squealed with delight as the furry grey squirrel rushed through the field.

The thief felt queasy as he heard the dog.

As the lady was ill she thought it was the fault of either the sausages or the jelly she had for tea.

Exercise 17

Clear all tabs. Now set new tab stops 20 and 40 characters along from the left-hand margin. Type the following exercise line by line, pressing the tab key between columns.

Sarah	yellow	Thursday
Julie	rose	Saturday
Hilary	red	Tuesday
Lee	white	Tuesday
Rohit	red	Friday
Stuart	grey	Saturday

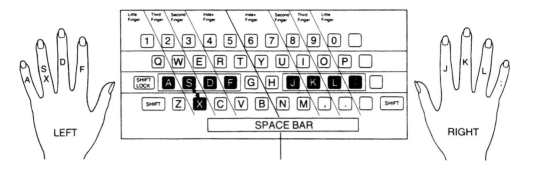

Exercise 22   New Letter x

sxs sxs sxs sxs sxs sxs sxs sxs

sax axe lax fox six fix
hex tax rex wax cox mix

flux text next oxen axis flax
Xmas foxy exit coax lynx exam

exist exact extra exalt exude excel
sixth fixed calyx index axiom exile

The sixth series of examinations commences next week.
Six extra examples are for examination on page sixty of the
text.

The texture of the textile was like foxskin.

The exact age of the sphinx was fixed at six thousand
years.

The text of the latest scroll was not exact when compared
with the excellent scripts dating from the time of the exile.

Key x   37

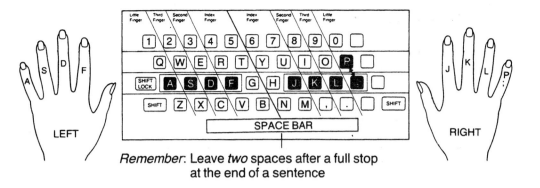

Remember: Leave *two* spaces after a full stop
at the end of a sentence

Exercise 18   New Letter p

;p; ;p; ;p; ;p; ;p; ;p; ;p; ;p;

pal pea pat pit pot pay
ape rip lap sup hip gap

post plug pest pray play pass
stop flap quip ship heep slap

Europe please pretty plaque repast

Please pass the pepper pot Peter.
People pushed past the pretty girl.
Please peel the apples ready for the pie.
She used her typewriter to type the replies to her letters.

    As we walked quietly through the fir wood our quarry
eluded us. He was at the top of the poplar tree quite out
of sight.

Extra Practice

win tin fen pin fun sun
end nor non ant ten now

money women runny nomad panda nasty
hyena minus niche rayon young snake

minimal passion mineral ranging tonnage
penalty transit stipend thicken persons

relinquish newsmonger occasional persuasion

Set the tabulator stops at 15, 30 and 45 characters from the left-hand margin and type the following:

Nicola	Tom	James	Connie
Yasmin	Kim	Walter	Lars
Emily	William	Sami	Jeremy
Fallon	Ian	Yan	Quenton

Extra Practice

```
paw hop pet tip put pie
asp ply dip pew pup rap

peat past pert ploy prey ship
rope jeep hope gasp wasp trip

apples ripple pushed passed gasped
pleats equips prefer gospel parade
```

All the people gasped as he slapped her.
After the party Paul put the paper plates away.
Pat had hoped to equip all the jeeps with rope.
The professor preferred to go to Europe for his trip.
The prototype of the purple quadruped was prepared for Paul.

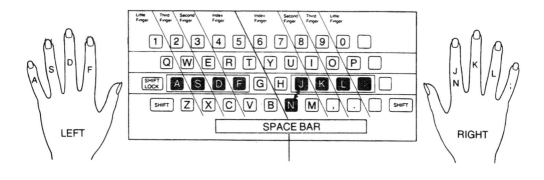

Exercise 21   New Letter n

jmj jnj jmj jnj jmj jnj jmj jnj
jnj jnj jnj jnj jnj jnj jnj jnj

and fan nod man any can
one won net run hen men

none nine nana neat note name
then plan down wine gone line
want inch tone nine lean cone

cannot dinner runner annual manner
quinsy adjoin squint rejoin jangle

intrinsic reconcile reckoning sprinkler
fighting laughing croaking stroking claiming

Neal and Noel went to the train station on Wednesday.

    Central heating installations are found in most modern
homes in England.

    Tina and Natasha had arranged a holiday in Scotland.
It was there that they planned to start lessons in skiing.

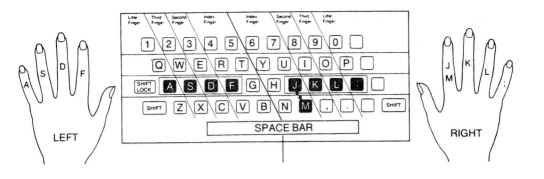

Exercise 19   New Letter m

jmj jmj jmj jmj jmj jmj jmj jmj

jam dim map mew him may
gym imp ham rim met sum

jump them some make drum game
mill army mope germ more poem

medal small prime misty mouse
thump flame remit moral mirth

Mark misread the word lump for hump.
All mortals make mistakes from time to time.

Indent the first lines, using the tabulator, five characters from the left-hand margin.

The weather was misty yet it was summer time.

The farmer sold his malt at the market for a modest fee.
He felt happy as he set off for home.

Why the mother asked for meat at the mill was a mystery.
Perhaps she thought it was Palmers.

Indent the start of each line by five characters from the left-hand margin.

The grocer sold the cauliflowers at a low price for a quick sale.

Sometimes it is difficult to choose a career whilst still at school or college.

The commercial course at college studied credit cards as well as cheque cards.

They had supper at a little cafe where they could see the sea. As well as the good food they were pleased at the sight of the ships.

Extra Practice

cow coy cue cap cot car
cam sac ice cue act cud

peck hock claw tick chic camp

caddy quack watch quick cough curry

cheque school jackal choose rocket

curiosity difficult quicklime copyright
Christmas calorific crocodile collector

Clare asked for a watch for Christmas.
All pupils must practise to aid success.

Each case of rice purchased this week is cut price.
The child came to the school office to collect her commerce file.

Extra Practice

mew yam mow mad mum gum
mam aim rum mat gem met

miss sump doom meat lump mask
perm most mild room mode lime

quorum market mature remiss mother
homage mostly summer farmer modest

trimmer mistake remorse mystery mislead

His mother may make him eat the meal at home.
The milkmaid worked at the farm three days per week.

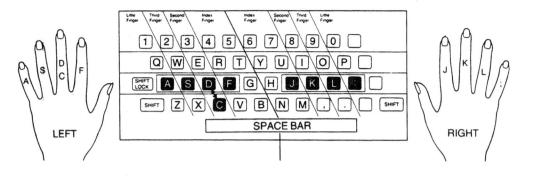

Exercise 20   New Letter c

dcd dcd dcd dcd dcd dcd dcd dcd

cad cod col cup cry cop
arc ice act roc ace tic

came fact come lace clam jack
pick hack mice code crew pact

touch cedar track child cress peach
cadet cello cider cocoa curly chest

chemical chromium creditor misplace clerical
commerce placates recourse practice macerate
